OUR SOLAR SYSTEM

Neptune

BY DANA MEACHEN RAU

Content Adviser: Dr. Stanley P. Jones, Assistant Director, Washington, D.C., Operations, NASA Classroom of the Future

Science Adviser: Terrence E. Young Jr., M.Ed., M.L.S., Jefferson Parish (La.) Public Schools

Reading Adviser: Dr. Linda D. Labbo, Department of Reading Education, College of Education, The University of Georgia

COMPASS POINT BOOKS

MINNEAPOLIS, MINNESOTA

Compass Point Books
3722 West 50th Street, #115
Minneapolis, MN 55410

Visit Compass Point Books on the Internet at *www.compasspointbooks.com*
or e-mail your request to *custserv@compasspointbooks.com*

Photographs ©: NASA, cover, 1, 3, 8–9, 11, 14; Astronomical Society of the Pacific, 4–5, 16, 17, 18, 19, 23;
Hulton/Archive by Getty Images, 6, 12–13; Adam Woolfitt/Corbis, 7; PhotoDisc, 10, 21 (top right);
Corbis, 20–21; Roger Ressmeyer/Corbis, 22; Courtesy of NASA/JPL/Caltech, 24–25.

Editors: E. Russell Primm and Emily J. Dolbear
Photo Researcher: Svetlana Zhurkina
Photo Selector: Dana Meachen Rau
Designer: The Design Lab
Illustrator: Graphicstock

Library of Congress Cataloging-in-Publication Data

Rau, Dana Meachen, 1971–
    Neptune / by Dana Meachen Rau.
        p. cm. — (Our solar system)
    Includes index.
    Summary: Briefly describes the surface features, internal composition,
    orbit, moons, and efforts to study the planet Neptune.
    ISBN 0-7565-0296-9 (hardcover)
    1. Neptune (Planet)—Juvenile literature. [1. Neptune (Planet)] I. Title.
    QB691 .R38 2002
    523.48'1—dc21   2002002946

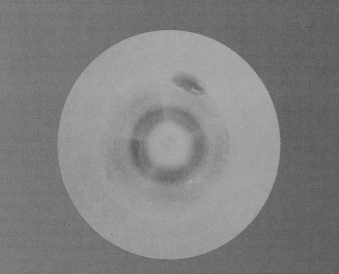

Table of Contents

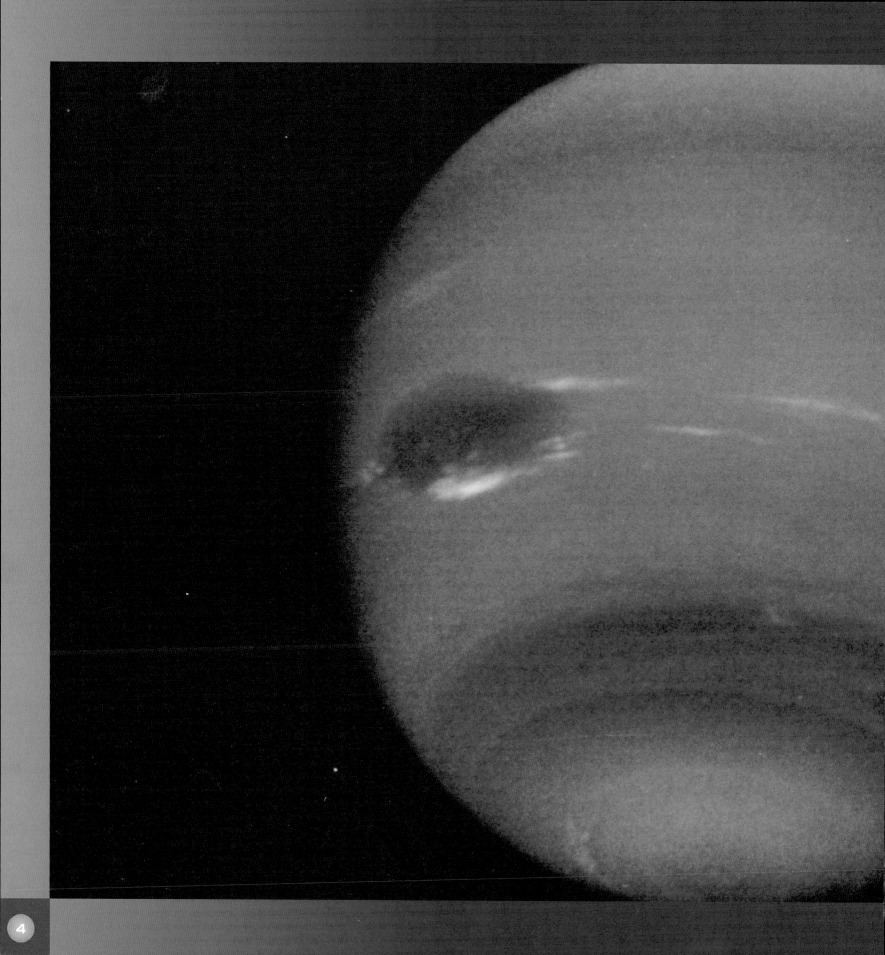

Looking at Neptune from Earth

Have you ever been outside on a very windy day? Did you fly a kite? Now imagine how strong the strongest winds in the whole **solar system** would be. You can find these strong winds on the planet Neptune. Some windy storms on Neptune stretch across an area as wide as Earth!

Neptune is the eighth planet from the Sun. People discovered the first seven planets by looking into the sky. Neptune, however, is not

◀ *Neptune looks like a blue circle in space.*

easy to see from Earth. You need **binoculars** or a **telescope**. Even then, Neptune looks like a small blue circle. So Neptune was discovered in a different way. Scientists had to use math to find Neptune.

Uranus is the seventh planet from the Sun. It was discovered in 1781. People studied the way it moved in the sky. They noticed that it moved differently from the way other planets moved. They thought another planet must be making Uranus move in this odd way.

In the 1840s, British **astronomer** John Couch Adams and

John Couch Adams (1819–1892) was one of the men who figured out Neptune's location in the sky. ▶

French astronomer Jean Leverrier (1811–1877) used math to figure out where this other planet should be. Then, in 1846, German astronomer Johann Gottfried Galle (1812–1910) found Neptune in the sky using their locations. He used the location that Leverrier had suggested.

Neptune was named after the Roman god of the sea. The god Neptune was known for making the sea dangerous by creating large storms and earthquakes. Perhaps people chose the name *Neptune* because its blue color made them think of the ocean.

◀ *The Roman god Neptune ruled over the sea.*

Looking at the Way Neptune Moves

All planets travel around the Sun, or revolve, in paths called orbits. One trip around the Sun is the length of a planet's year. Neptune takes almost 165 Earth-years to make this trip. People have known about Neptune for about 150 years. Neptune hasn't made even one trip around the Sun since it was discovered.

As Neptune revolves around the Sun, it also spins, or rotates. One rotation is a planet's day. One day on Earth

Half of Neptune is lit by the Sun while the other half is in shadow. ▶

is about twenty-four hours long. On Neptune, one day is only a little more than sixteen hours.

Neptune is usually the eighth planet. For 20 out of every 248 Earth-years, however, it is the ninth planet from the Sun. That happens because the planet Pluto has a strange orbit. Pluto's orbit sometimes takes it inside the orbit of Neptune. So, from 1979 to 1999, Neptune—not Pluto—was the farthest plan-et from the Sun.

Neptune has different seasons as it orbits the Sun. Each season lasts about forty-one years. The very top and very bottom parts of the planet are called **poles**.

During summer at each pole, the Sun is always out in the sky. It doesn't set at night. That means the Sun is out for forty-one years. That is one long summer!

Neptune spins as it orbits the Sun. One ▼ rotation, or day, takes about sixteen hours.

The south pole of Neptune ▸▸

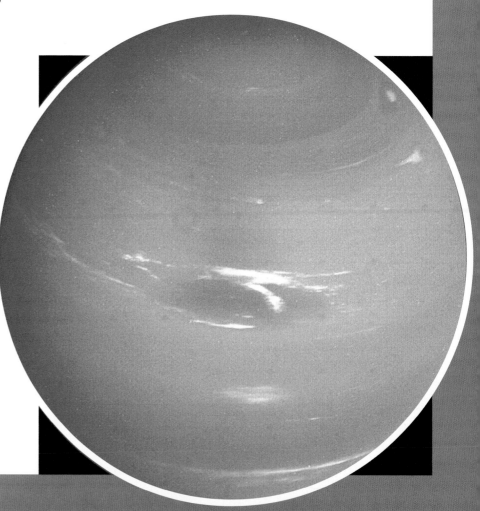

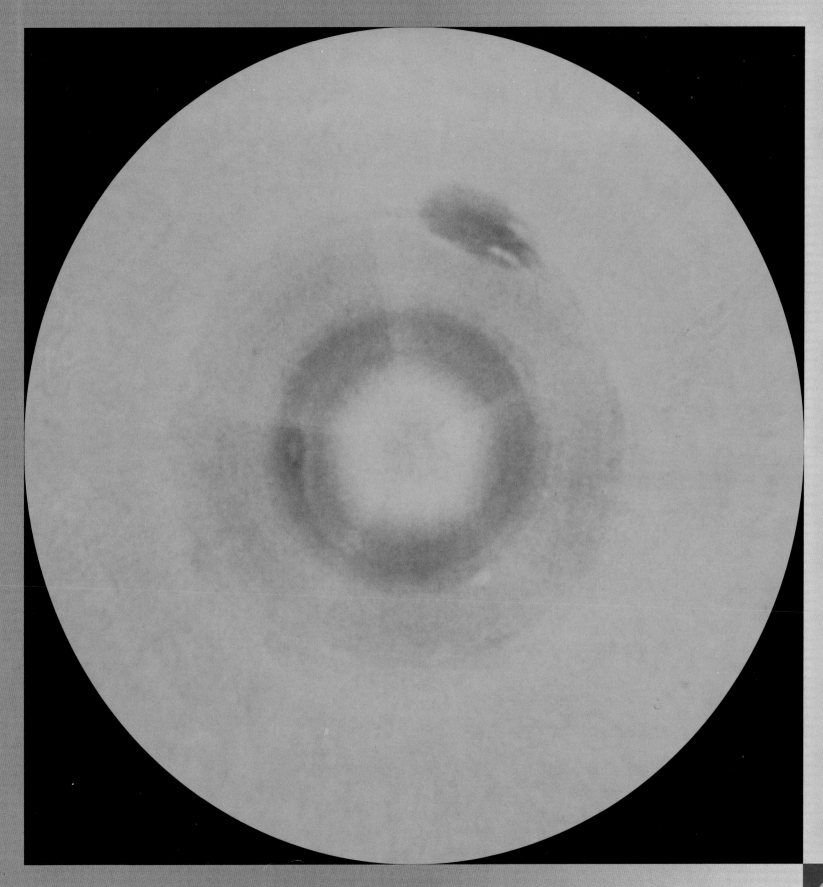

Looking Through Neptune

⭐ Neptune does not have a solid surface like Earth does. It is a gas giant planet. Jupiter, Saturn, and Uranus are also gas giants. They are made up of mostly gases and ice.

Neptune looks blue because it has a gas called methane in its atmosphere. A planet's atmosphere is made up of the gases around it. Neptune's atmosphere is mostly made up of hydrogen and helium. Hydrogen is one of the gases people breathe

Neptune is a gas giant planet made mostly ▶ of hydrogen and helium.

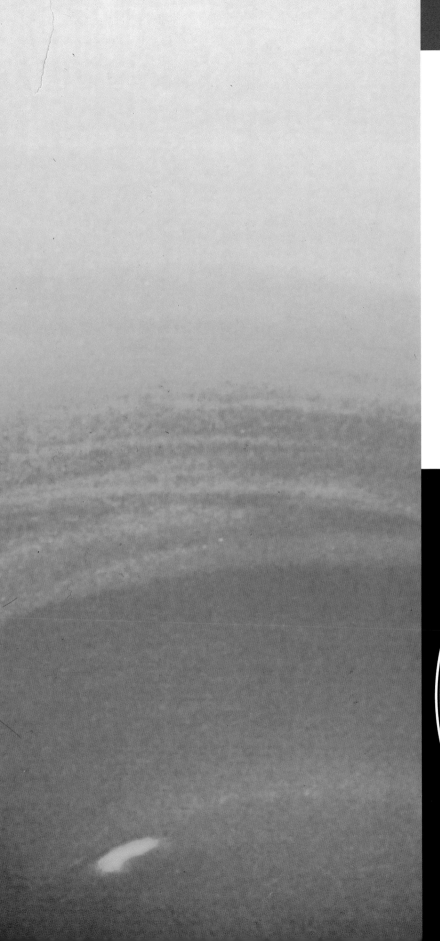

on Earth. Helium is the gas
people put in balloons to
make them float in the air.
Neptune's atmosphere is filled
with white clouds that circle
the planet. The temperature
of these long clouds is very
cold. The cloud tops are about
–330 degrees Fahrenheit

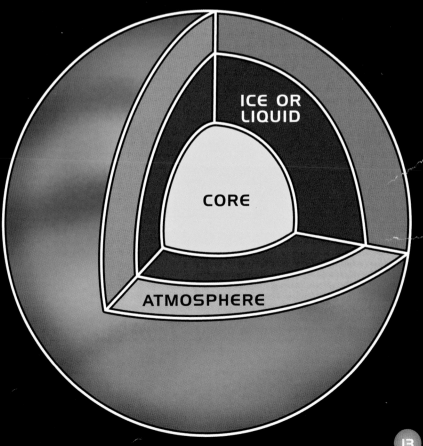

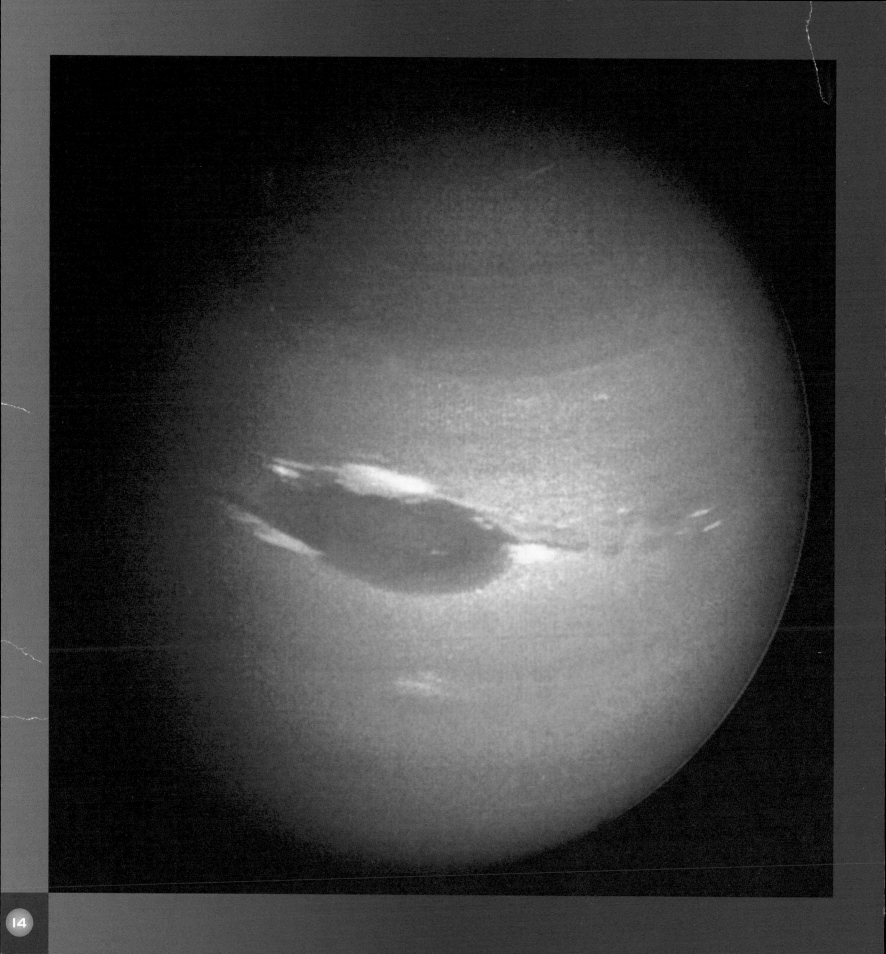

(–200 degrees Celsius).

Neptune's atmosphere is very thick and goes deep into the planet. After the atmosphere comes a layer of ice and liquid. Scientists believe Neptune probably has a hard rocky CORE. This core is about the same size as the planet Earth.

Neptune has the strangest winds of any planet. Storms have been found all through its atmosphere. One huge storm found in 1989 was called the Great Dark Spot. The winds of this storm blew up to 1,200 miles (1,930 kilometers) per hour. The Great Dark Spot was as large as Earth.

The Great Dark Spot has disappeared now. But in 1994, the Hubble Space Telescope found another spot. The Hubble Space Telescope is a giant telescope that orbits in space. It found a storm spot in the northern part of Neptune. These storm spots tell scientists that weather on Neptune changes all the time.

◄ *The Great Dark Spot was an enormous storm the size of Earth.*

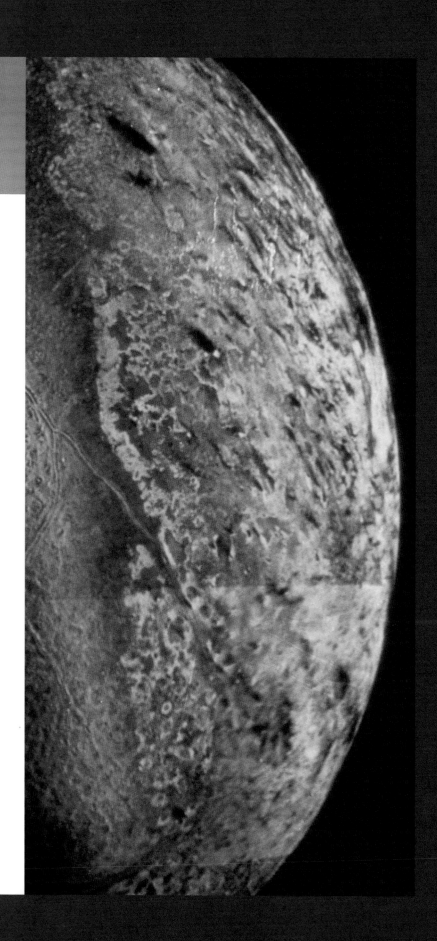

Looking Around Neptune

In 1846, British astronomer William Lassell found a moon orbiting Neptune. Scientists named it Triton. In ancient Greece, one of the sons of the Roman god Neptune was called Triton. In 1949, Gerard Kuiper discovered another moon, which was named Nereid. The spacecraft *Voyager 2* found six more moons. So Neptune now has eight known moons.

Triton is Neptune's largest moon. It is one of the most interesting objects in the solar

Triton is the coldest place in the ▶ solar system.

system. The moon Triton orbits Neptune in a direction opposite to the planet. It is almost the size of Earth's Moon. Its southern hemisphere appears pink with dark patches and long grooves. **Volcanoes** cover Triton. They are not like volcanoes on Earth. They do not shoot out hot **lava**. Instead, they shoot out cold nitrogen gas and dark dust particles. Triton is colder than any other object in the solar system. The temperature on Triton is –400° Fahrenheit (–240° Celsius). That is colder than Neptune itself.

Neptune also has rings.

◄ *The surface of Triton*

The rings on the planet Saturn are large and easy to see. Scientists had a hard time seeing Neptune's rings from Earth. *Voyager 2* took very clear pictures of them. It found four rings around the planet. Scientists do not know what they are made of. They may be pieces of rock. Some of these pieces are large. Scientists believe that most are very small, dust-sized pieces. Patches in the rings are brighter than other parts. And some parts of the rings clump together. The cause of the clumping is not known.

Three views of Neptune's rings. The ▶ ▶▶ *two views on the opposite page are very long time-exposure photos taken by* Voyager 2.

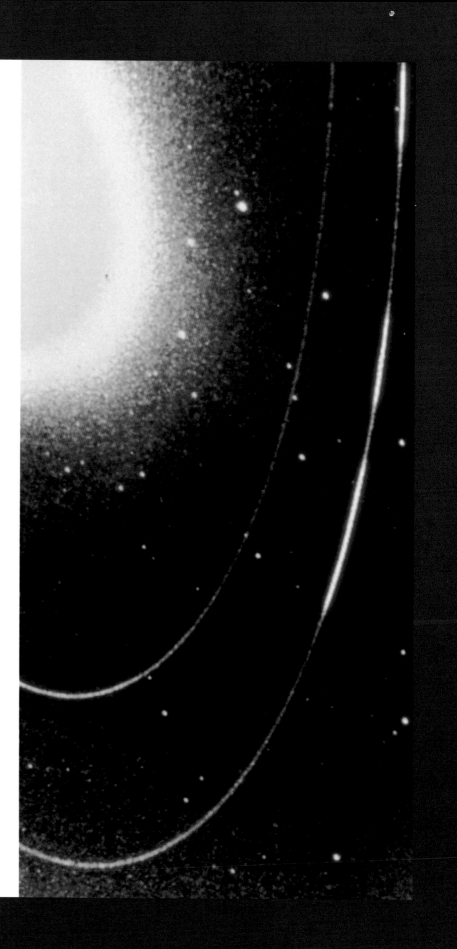

Looking at Neptune from Space

Voyager 2 is the only spacecraft to have visited Neptune. Most of what scientists know about the planet comes from *Voyager 2*'s mission. *Voyager 2* studied all four gas giant planets. It was launched from Earth on August 20, 1977. That launch date was chosen because the planets were very close to each other at that time. The spacecraft could fly by all of them.

Scientists would have been happy if *Voyager 2* had flown

The spacecraft Voyager 2 *was sent on a* ▶ *mission to the gas giant planets.*

by only Jupiter and Saturn. The spacecraft was built to last five years. After visiting Jupiter and Saturn, however, *Voyager 2* was still working well. It went on to study Uranus and Neptune.

▲ Voyager 2 *was built to study only Jupiter and Saturn. It was in such good shape, though, that it flew on to Uranus (right) and Neptune (left).*

Voyager 2 flew by Neptune in August 1989. By that time, it had been traveling for twelve years. *Voyager* 2 was so far away that the facts it sent back to Earth took four hours to get here. It sent back thousands of pictures of Neptune, its moons, and its rings.

Voyager 2's mission continued even after it studied Neptune. It is now traveling into deep space and away from the Sun. Scientists have no idea what it will find. They expect the spacecraft to last until about 2020.

Voyager 2 *sent pictures back to Earth for scientists to study.* ▲

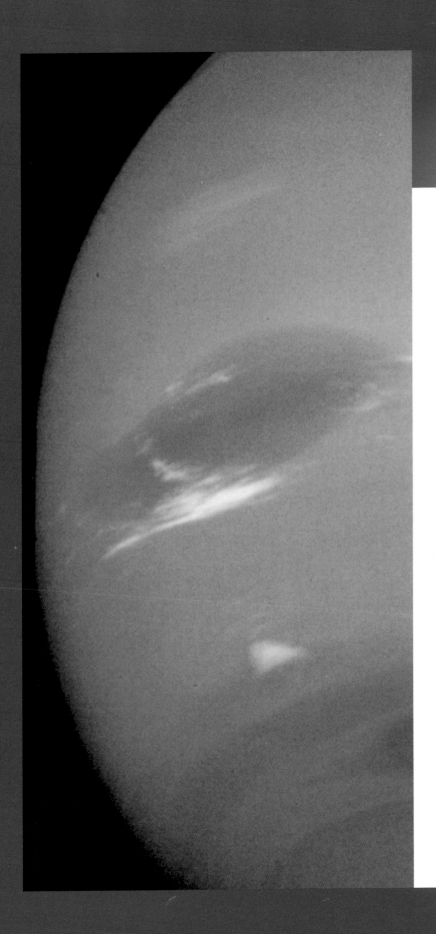

Looking to the Future

✦ The only facts scientists have today about Neptune came from one spacecraft. So they still have many questions. They want to learn more about the strong winds. They want to know what happened to the Great Dark Spot. They hope to plan another mission to the planet.

Scientists want to know more about Triton, too. They are interested in Triton because of the way it orbits

◀ *Scientists still have many questions about Neptune and its stormy, windy atmosphere.*

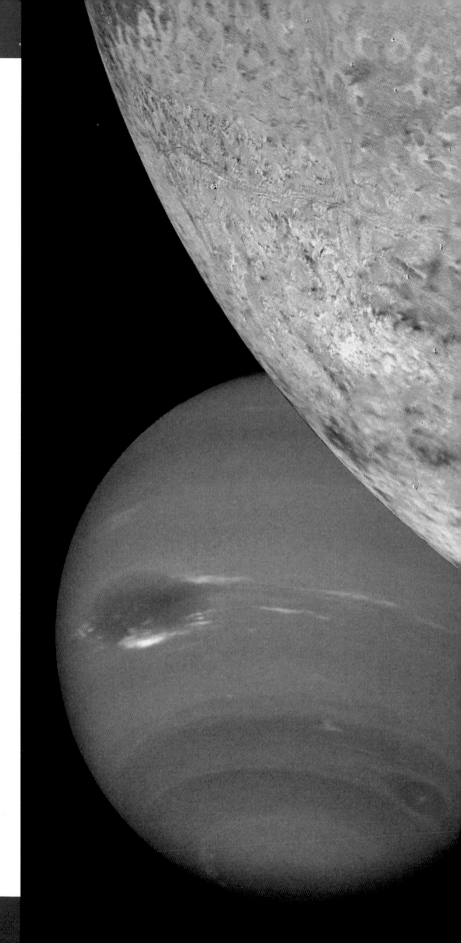

Neptune. It is slowly getting closer and closer to the planet. One day it may crash into it. Or it may break up into pieces. That might form more rings. It may not happen for millions of years!

It takes a long time for changes to take place in space. Scientists like to think about the future and how planets change. They will keep looking closely at the faraway planet Neptune.

Triton is an interesting moon. ▶

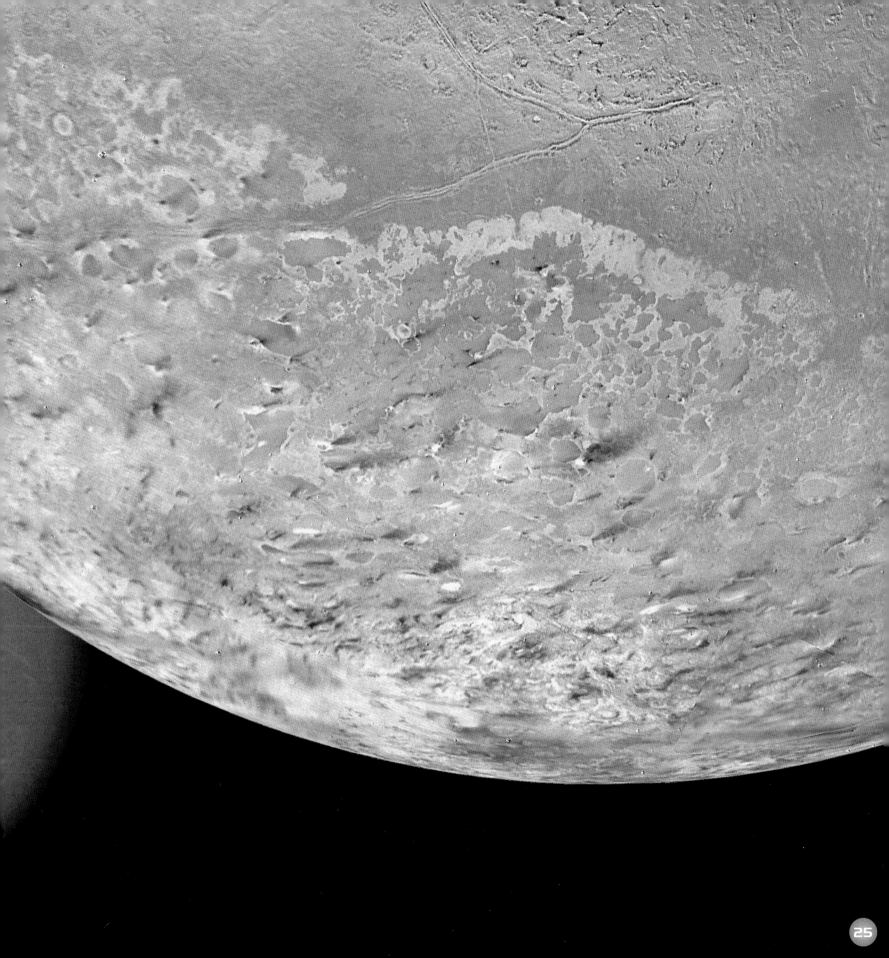

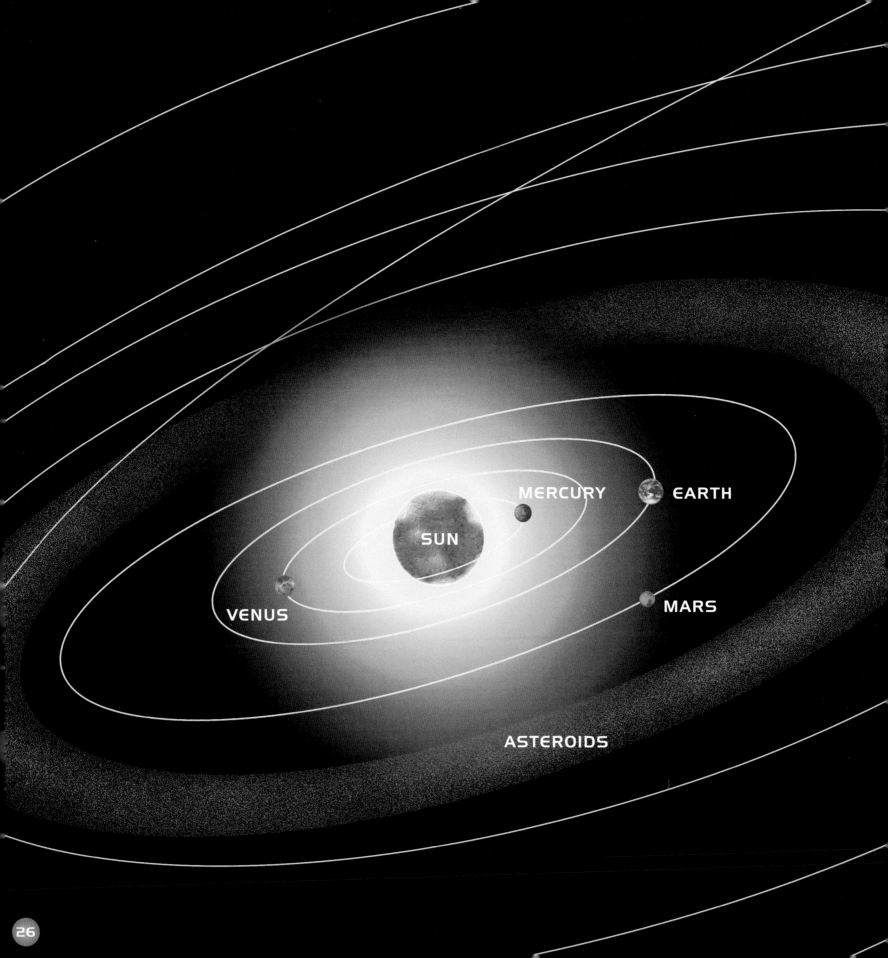

SUN

MERCURY

EARTH

VENUS

MARS

ASTEROIDS

JUPITER

URANUS

SATURN

NEPTUNE

PLUTO

Glossary

astronomer—someone who studies space

binoculars—a tool, like a high-powered pair of glasses, that makes objects look closer

core—the center of a planet

lava—liquid rock

poles—the northernmost and southernmost points on a planet

solar system—a group of objects in space including the Sun, planets, moons, asteroids, comets, and meteoroids

telescope—a tool astronomers use to make objects look closer

temperature—how hot or cold something is

volcanoes—mountains that may erupt with hot liquid rock or hot gas; on Triton they shoot out cold gas and dust particles

A Neptune Flyby

Neptune is the fourth-largest planet and the eighth planet from the Sun when Pluto is not inside its orbit.

If you weighed 75 pounds (34 kilograms) on Earth, you would weigh 82 pounds (37 kilograms) on Neptune.

Average distance from the Sun: 2.8 billion miles (4.5 billion kilometers)

Distance from Earth: 2,676 million miles (4,687 million kilometers) to 2,913 million miles (4,687 million kilometers)

Diameter: 30,775 miles (49,528 kilometers)

Number of times Earth would fit inside Neptune: almost 58

Did You Know?

- Some people think *Neptune* is the perfect name for the planet. The god Neptune was often angry and had a bad temper, much like the planet's harsh stormy weather.

- It takes Neptune almost 165 years to travel around the Sun. It has not made a full orbit since it was discovered in 1846.

- *Voyager 2* traveled 42,000 miles (67,578 kilometers) per hour to reach Neptune.

- As of summer 2002, *Voyager 2* had traveled more than 13 billion miles (21 billion kilometers).

- *Voyager 2* spotted a cloud zooming around Neptune. Scientists called the cloud "Scooter."

- Triton is similar in size and appearance to the planet Pluto.

- The "ice" volcanoes on Triton shoot invisible nitrogen gas and dark dust particles into the sky for several miles.

Time it takes to orbit around Sun (one Neptune year): 164.79 Earth-years

Time it takes to rotate (one Neptune day): 16.11 Earth-hours

Structure: rocky/iron core, liquid/icy layer, gases

Average temperature of clouds: –330° Fahrenheit (–200° Celsius)

Atmosphere: hydrogen, helium, methane

Atmospheric pressure (Earth=1.0): unknown

Moons: 8

Rings: 4

Want to Know More?

AT THE LIBRARY

Kerrod, Robin. *Uranus, Neptune, and Pluto.* Minneapolis: Lerner Publications, 2000.

Mitton, Jacqueline, and Simon Mitton. *Scholastic Encyclopedia of Space.* New York: Scholastic Reference, 1998.

Redfern, Martin. *The Kingfisher Young People's Book of Space.* New York: Kingfisher, 1998.

Ridpath, Ian. *Stars and Planets.* New York: DK Publishing, Inc., 1998.

Simon, Seymour. *Neptune.* New York: William Morrow, 1999.

ON THE WEB

Exploring the Planets: Neptune
http://www.nasm.edu/ceps/etp/neptune/
For more information about Neptune

The Grandest Tour
http://www.jpl.nasa.gov/voyager/
For more information about the Voyager missions

The Nine Planets: Neptune
http://www.seds.org/nineplanets/nineplanets/neptune.html
For a multimedia tour of Neptune

Solar System Exploration: Neptune
http://sse.jpl.nasa.gov/features/planets/neptune/neptune.html
For more information about Neptune and its features

Space Kids
http://spacekids.hq.nasa.gov
NASA's space-science site designed just for kids

Space.com
http://www.space.com
For the latest news about everything to do with space

Star Date Online: Neptune
http://www.stardate.org/resources/ssguide/neptune.html
For an overview of Neptune and hints on where it can be seen in the sky

Welcome to the Planets: Neptune
http://pds.jpl.nasa.gov/planets/choices/neptune1.htm
For pictures and information about Neptune

THROUGH THE MAIL

Goddard Space Flight Center
Code 130, Public Affairs Office
Greenbelt, MD 20771
To learn more about space exploration

Jet Propulsion Laboratory
4800 Oak Grove Drive
Pasadena, CA 91109
To learn more about the spacecraft
missions

Lunar and Planetary Institute
3600 Bay Area Boulevard
Houston, TX 77058
To learn more about Neptune and
other planets

Space Science Division
NASA Ames Research Center
Moffet Field, CA 94035
To learn more about Neptune and
solar system exploration

ON THE ROAD

**Adler Planetarium and
Astronomy Museum**
1300 S. Lake Shore Drive
Chicago, IL 60605-2403
312/922-STAR
To visit the oldest planetarium
in the Western Hemisphere

***Exploring the Planets* and
*Where Next Columbus?***
National Air and Space Museum
7th and Independence Avenue, S.W.
Washington, DC 20560
202/357-2700
To learn more about the solar system
at this museum exhibit

**Rose Center for Earth and
Space/Hayden Planetarium**
Central Park West at 79th Street
New York, NY 10024-5192
212/769-5100
To visit this new planetarium and
learn more about the planets

UCO/Lick Observatory
University of California
Santa Cruz, CA 95064
408/274-5061
To see the telescope that was used to
discover the first planets outside of
our solar system

Index

◀ **About the Author:** *Dana Meachen Rau loves to study space. Her office walls are covered with pictures of planets, astronauts, and spacecraft. She also likes to look up at the sky with her telescope and write poems about what she sees. Ms. Rau is the author of more than seventy-five books for children, including nonfiction, biographies, storybooks, and early readers. She lives in Burlington, Connecticut, with her husband, Chris, and children, Charlie and Allison.*